The Sw

by Richard Bate

LIBRARY OF CONGRESS CATALOGING – IN – PUBLICATION DATA

Bate, Richard
The Sweeper

ISBN No. 1-890946-30-3
Library of Congress Catalog Card Number 99-074795
Copyright © August 1999

Reedswain Books are available at specail discounts for bulk purchase. For details, contact Reedswain at 1-800-331-5191.

Art Direction and Layout
Kimberly N. Bender

Editing and Proofing
Bryan R. Beaver

Printing by
DATA REPRODUCTIONS
Auburn Hills, Michigan

REEDSWAIN INC.
612 Pughtown Road
Spring City PA 19475
1-800-331-5191 • www.reedswain.com

The Sweeper

by Richard Bate

Published by
REEDSWAIN INC.

Foreword

The deployment of a center back in a relatively free role has never found favor in English soccer; our game has suffered because of that omission. Few teachers or coaches understand the sweeper's role or his responsibilities and fewer still appreciate his opportunities for creative play. Having a 'free' player in any phase of the game is vital if attacking play is to be developed intelligently and skillfully.

This book will be of enormous value to those teachers, coaches and players who want to take our game forward out of the shackles of negative, attritional styles of play. There are not many of us about!

Allen Wade

PLAYING WITH A SWEEPER

What is a sweeper?

Defensively?
1. A player who gives the team a numerical advantage in our defending organization.
2. Operates from a position generally between the goalkeeper and rear defenders.
3. Operates frequently from a position <u>behind the designated 'markers'</u> in the defensive structure, but may also position himself <u>amongst</u> the markers and <u>ahead</u> of the markers as circumstances demand.
4. A player <u>without</u> a specific or designated <u>marking role</u> although he may be required to mark opponents in certain circumstances.
5. A player who a team wishes to use in a 'free-from-marking' role, in a covering, <u>communicating and organizational</u> function.
6. A player who on demand <u>takes over</u> other defending functions from this free role when compelled to and <u>knows when to do so.</u>

The sweeper only moves out from the covering and organizing role when gaining possession is almost certain, the threat to goal is serious or he can significantly delay attacking momentum while co-defenders recover position.

Offensively
1. A player who can <u>initiate</u> and <u>participate in attacks</u> from the defending third of the field.
2. A player who can <u>progress the play</u> into midfield areas by carrying the ball, possibly combining with other players to move possession into midfield areas and beyond.
3. A player who <u>recognizes</u> when to move into positions ahead of the back line in order to receive passes to progress the play.
4. A player who <u>takes over the role of other defenders</u> or organizes the take-over of those roles when they move forward in possession or to support the play.

QUALITIES OF A SWEEPER

Offensively	Defensively
1. Understand how, where and when to support the play around him. 2. 'Read' the play around him before and on receiving possession to assess circumstances and possibilities. 3. Has assured controlling, running with the ball and passing skills and knows how and when to use those skills. 4. Can influence the position and role of those around him by giving information or by decisive action. 5. Is prepared to and capable of moving forward from his rear position to contribute to attacking play in possession and also when he is not in possession but is highly likely to receive the ball.	1. Understands when and where to position himself according to the movement of the ball and opponents possibly marked by his teammates. 2. Recognizes when to change roles from sweeper to marker, pressure player, etc. 3. Can understand and organize teammates to counter opposition attacking threats. 4. Consistently and accurately 'reads the play' as it is developing – a defensive controller. 5. Appreciates risk, priority and therefore takes no unnecessary chances in the defensive third.

FUNCTIONS OF THE SWEEPER

From his position behind the defense a sweeper's main functions will include:

1. Being the chief 'defensive controller' by:
    a. Communicating verbally with co-defenders.
    b. Verbally organizing co-defenders in their responsibilities and functions.
    c. Initiating pre-planned defensive reactions to known situations, e.g. Baresi of AC Milan: he controls the defense, pushing out quickly to catch opponents offside.

2. Reading the Play
    a. Position himself to do so.
    b. Observe movements and actions of opponents and the ball.
    c. Move or organize others to move and counter any necessary threats.
    d. Prioritize the actions of himself and co-defenders.

3. Accepting a variety of different defensive roles and understanding when to change roles
    a. Free player – ball ahead, ball wide, ball in the attacking third, ball in the midfield third?
    b. Marking responsibility.
    c. Cover teammates.
    d. Leave the middle areas to pressure the ball, intercept passes.
    e. Track and eventually mark opponents moving to receive possession.

4. Gaining possession of the ball and initiating attacking play
    a. From interceptions.
    b. From challenges.
    c. From teammates.

POSITIONING AND OPERATING ROLES

A Sweeper's Area of Operation

A guideline to assist sweeper and coach

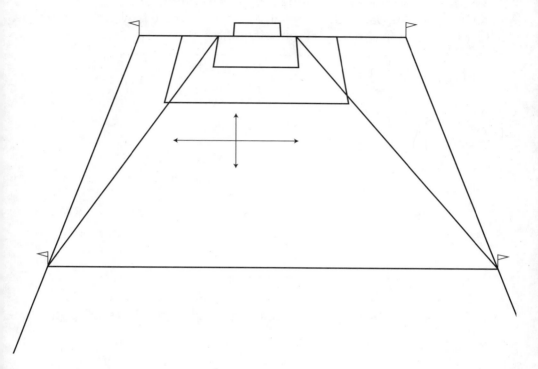

The sweeper's area of operation usually involves him in playing a defensive role as the rear-most defender. A useful guideline to assist a sweeper or the sweeper's coach is to identify the area of operation as a funnel leading from the half-way line flag to the corner of the penalty box on each side of the pitch. That is not to say that a sweeper will not come outside that area but if he does, it is usually as a result of an error made by teammates ahead of him or the near certainty of an interception that causes him to defend outside this space or the near certainty of an interception. It is fair to say that the majority of the sweepers defending functions will take place inside this funnel: within this area the sweeper needs to co-ordinate his positioning and activity with all teammates but specifically the 'markers' and the goalkeeper. Obviously activity, roles and responsibilities are continually changing with circumstances but co-ordinating a sweepers role with those of the markers and the goalkeeper is particularly vital.

Guidelines to Assist the Sweeper in his Functions

Positioning

1. The sweeper should remember to position himself:

   a. between the ball and the penalty spot – when the play is ahead/in front of him and in the 'funnel' of defending.

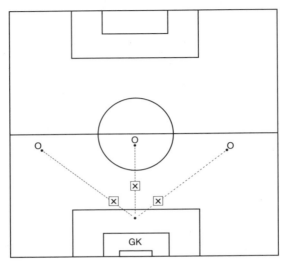

   b. between the ball and 6 yard line when ball is in a wide 1/3 position.

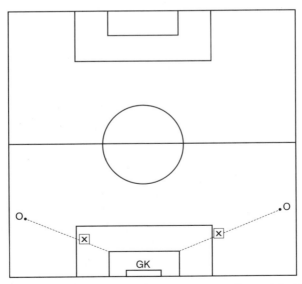

As the <u>location</u> of the ball <u>changes,</u> so the sweeper <u>adjusts</u> his position accordingly providing he remains a free player and not involved in marking duties. <u>The above guidelines (and they are only that) will help a sweeper to position himself.</u>

Further influences on a sweeper's position will be:
1. The distance the ball is away from goal.
2. The playing situation, e.g. attackers' movements having broken free of markers.
3. The position of the goalkeeper.

1. The distance the ball is away from goal

Example. If the ball is in our attacking third then the sweeper can move the defense forward up to the halfway line and take his position alongside the other back defenders or slightly behind them. If he does not 'compress' the team shape, the opponents may stretch our team and create more space for themselves to play in when gaining possession. Space and time is usually to the attacking team's advantage.

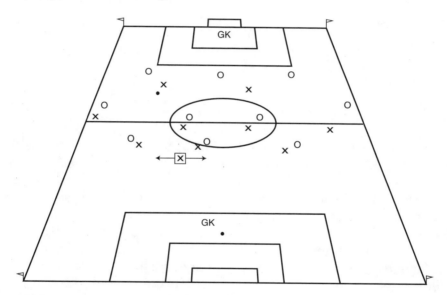

From this distance the ball is unlikely to be delivered behind the defense to cause an imminent problem to the team and should there be any indication that such a pass will be delivered the sweeper and his fellow defenders can:
1. Drop towards their own goal quickly to reduce the chance of the ball being received by an attacker, behind the defending line.
2. Hold a defending line, refuse to drop back or even move forward in a co-ordinated rehearsed manner to trap opponents offside.

By 'compressing the play' and reducing distances between front and back lines, the opposition have less space in which to operate and 'pressuring' as a tactic by the defending team is likely to become more effective.

The Playing Situation

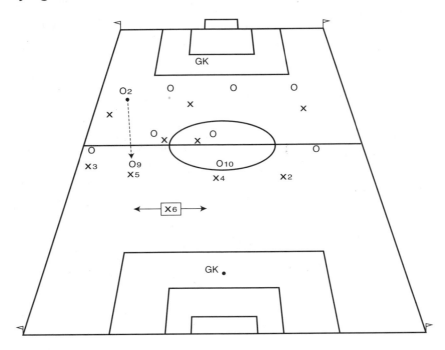

If the opposition have possession of the ball in their defending middle third of the field then the sweeper's role will be to provide cover or security for tight marking defenders ahead of him. The sweeper's position will be between the ball and the penalty spot and approximately 10 to 15 yards behind markers X5 and X4. Strikers O9 and O10 are likely to move into support positions to receive passes from rear defenders, e.g. O2. They should be tightly marked by defenders whose positioning and movements will largely be dictated by the strikers' actions. The sweeper places himself in such a position that if he does not deter passes from being delivered behind the defense, he can move to intercept any passes played beyond rear defenders. On moving to cut-out any passes made behind the defenders he may have to decide how to act on a time/situation basis and gain possession to create attacks, play safely as required if under pressure, or pass back to and support the goalkeeper as necessary. The distance of 10 - 15 yards behind the nearest marker in the situation as shown is approximate and will vary from player to player and team to team. However, from this distance, the sweeper can move to intercept passes beyond markers, read the play as it develops, collect any 'free' runners to the back of the defense and can communicate and organize the team ahead of him. A basic guideline for the sweeper in this situation is not to 'sweep' beyond the distance that the ball can be delivered.

The Playing Situation

If the opposition have possession of the ball in the attacking middle third, the sweeper need not position himself any deeper than the edge of the penalty area and should be in a position to assist other defenders who are in need of support and be able to move forward to defend as needed (see below).

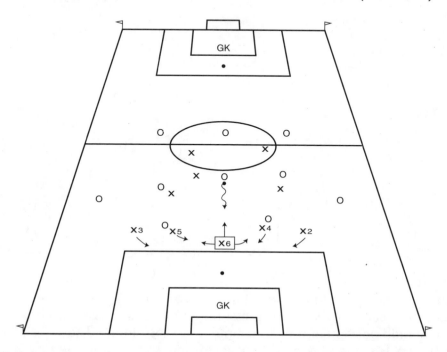

The goalkeeper should be ready and prepared to cover the space between himself and the sweeper should the ball be delivered there within his range of operation and also other defenders will cover and mark any opponents who attempt to move into those spaces to receive passes. From the position shown in the diagram, the sweeper is able to come forward to meet any unopposed attacker who threatens the goal with the ball. The importance of an imaginary line of 35 yard radius from goal is explained later. From the position shown by the diagram, X6 can read the play and move quickly to pressure the ball, cover teammates, give information to teammates and also establish a 'line' for the defense beyond which any attackers would be in an offside position. The sweeper keeps in line with the ball and the penalty spot but is now 'flatter', not so deep behind markers, in his support position and relationships with co-defenders.

The Playing Situation

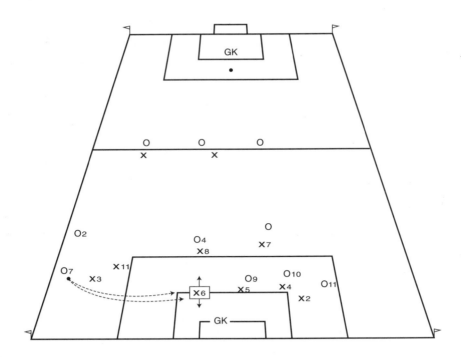

When the ball is in the attacking third, the sweeper, if not required to move out from the central position to pressure the player in possession or intercept passes, should position himself to counter any cross. In the diagram above, our flank-back X3 is opposed by O7 in possession and is supported by X11 our midfield player. In this situation, sweeper X6 can position himself to cut out any cross from O7 or O2. Providing that attackers in the penalty box are marked and no opponents are free and moving into the scoring areas, the sweeper should position himself just ahead of a line drawn from the near post to the edge of the penalty box and approximately six yards out from goal. From this position the sweeper may intercept crosses that are not high enough to reach far post areas and may also intercept hard, low driven crosses before they pass across the face of the goal. Once more, early and decisive communication from the goalkeeper is helpful in attending to the situation effectively as the cross is delivered. Should the ball be passed backwards by O7 to O2 then the sweeper may move forward, accompanied by his other defenders, possibly 4 or 5 yards depending on the time and the distance that the ball travels to O2. He may also move to cover teammates in 1 v 1 situations in the shooting areas and pressure the ball if needed, as it is moved across or around the edge of the penalty area.

The Playing Situation

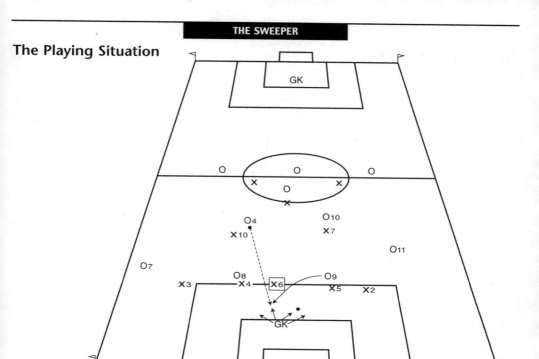

The <u>goalkeeper-sweeper relationship</u> is a crucial factor in any successful sweep-er system. <u>Verbal and positional relationships are vital</u> to establish and if suc-cessfully completed will avoid much confusion. The confusion arises when basic guidelines for performance are absent. In the situation shown above, the goalkeeper's position will be <u>around the edge of the 6 yard box</u>. If the sweep-er were to position himself say 10 yards behind X4 then both the goalkeeper and the sweeper would be so close to each other that if any pass was made into the penalty box, confusion as to responsibility for dealing with that threat may ensue. If the sweeper positions himself around the <u>edge of the penalty box</u> he can <u>support teammates exposed in 1 v 1 situations</u> in the scoring areas, come forward to pressure opponents if needed, <u>communicate</u> to teammates ahead of him and <u>read the play</u>. He can also, if needed, drop quickly into the penalty box to attend to any situation that is not dealt with by the goalkeep-er and co-defenders. The space between the goalkeeper and the rear defend-ers has to be regarded as the <u>goalkeeper's responsibility</u> in terms of his <u>com-municating</u> to others and <u>coming forward to intercept and gather passes</u> that are within his range. Angled passes away from the goalkeeper for attackers should be countered by markers but the goalkeeper should see the space between himself and his defenders as an area where he should come forward to gain possession early, wherever it is possible and appropriate to do so. Decisive communication and action will help resolve problems. If the goal-keeper is hesitant with communication and action then defenders must act decisively as they feel is appropriate.

The Importance of the 35 Yard Line

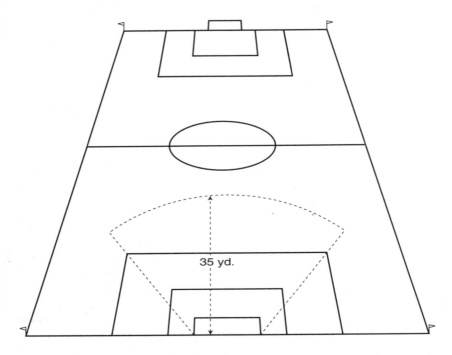

The overwhelming majority of goals are scored from within the penalty area, with an extremely high ratio scored from within 12 yards of goal. However, it is not unknown or impossible to score from ranges of up to 35 yards – goals have been scored from longer distances. Once opponents have possession of the ball within the area shown above, our defense must have as its <u>major aim the prevention of shooting opportunities</u> and reduction of potential shooting opportunities.

The sweeper plays a vital role in this by carrying out the following functions:

1. <u>Pressuring</u> from 2 - 3 yards any <u>opponent who is free</u> and in possession of the ball if no other defender is doing so within the 35 yard area.
2. <u>Sending</u> a fellow defender to pressure the ball and <u>take over</u> his marking responsibilities.
3. Moving to <u>cover any marker</u> in a 1 v 1 situation with an attacker, especially one opposed by an attacker, facing our goal within 35 yards of goal.
4. <u>Tracking</u> and eventually <u>marking</u> any opponent moving into a receiving position inside the goal-scoring area if no other teammate is doing so.

PROBLEM SITUATIONS

Favorable Situations to Assist the Sweeper

1. Ball is guided into central areas of the defending third of the pitch.

2. Midfield <u>marking and tracking roles are adhered to </u>and the sweeper is not drawn into a marking function.

3. <u>Rear markers maintain discipline and quality</u> in their marking and general defending roles and so sweepers do not need to take-over 'free' attackers breaking off markers.

4. <u>Pressure is applied</u> to players in possession of the ball and they are denied the freedom to select passes to receivers in high priority defending areas.

5. <u>Opposition defenders are restricted from breaking forward</u> into and beyond midfield areas to create situations where they create a numerical advantage around the ball.

Problem Situations for the Sweeper

<u>The following are situations that arise and may cause the sweeper to leave his position of 'security' behind the defense. Therefore we should seek to avoid these circumstances.</u>

1. Passes made behind the defense, especially in wide areas, to attackers who have broken free from markers (Diagram 1).

2. Players breaking away from markers, often from deep positions and moving unmarked to be potential receivers of passes in goal-scoring or goal-creating positions (Diagram 2).

3. Players breaking at goal in possession of the ball and moving into potential goal-scoring positions (Dia. 3).

4. Players breaking free into positions where they may create a goal-scoring opportunity, often in flank positions (Diagram 4).

5. Markers being attacked with the ball in 1 v 1 situations in or around the penalty area (Diagram 5).

6. A marking defender leaves his immediate opponent to counter a bigger threat (Diagram 6).

7. The opposition decide to position an attacker against our sweeper (Diagram 7).

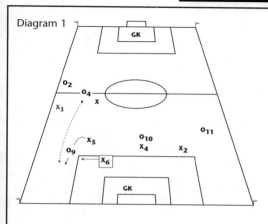

Diagram 1

1. <u>Passes made behind the defense into wide areas to attackers who have broken free from markers</u>

Situations

a. O4 (midfield) has passed the ball into the attacking third of the field into a position down the sides of the penalty box to O9 who has broken free from marker X5.

b. Sweeper X6 now has to leave his position centrally to cover the threat of O9 in the attacking third.

c. X5 should now recover goal-side of the ball as quickly as possible and replace the sweeper.

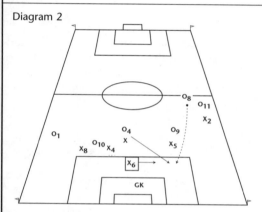

Diagram 2

2. <u>Players breaking away from markers who may be potential receivers of passes in goal-scoring or goal-creating areas</u>

Situations

a. O4 (midfield) has broken into the penalty box to receive from O8.

b. Sweeper X6 takes over the role of tracking and then marking O4 as he moves into a potential goal-scoring area.

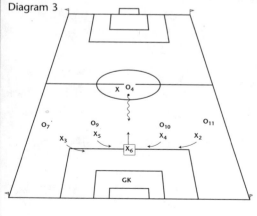

Diagram 3

3. <u>Players breaking at goal in possession of the ball and moving into potential goal-scoring positions</u>

Situations

a. O4 (midfield) running with the ball through midfield and to within 30 yards of goal.

b. X6 on O4 entering into an area with in 30 - 35 yards of goal, comes forward from his position behind rear defenders to oppose O4 in a 1 v 1 situation.

c. Defenders X4, X5, X2, X3 recover centrally to assist X6 in countering the threat.

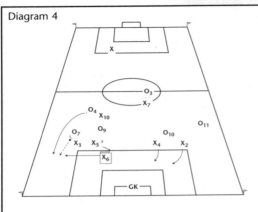

Diagram 4

4. <u>Players breaking free into positions where they may create a goal-scoring opportunity – often in flank positions</u>

Situations

a. O4 has broken free from X10 and has made an overlapping run past O7 to receive the ball.

b. X6 – on recognizing the situation moves from a covering position behind other defenders to mark and pressure O4 as he receives the ball.

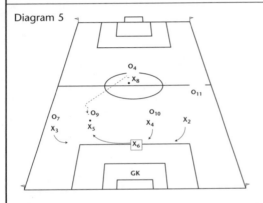

Diagram 5

5. <u>Markers being attacked in 1 v 1 situations around the penalty box</u>

Situations

a. O9 has turned on receiving possession from O4 and has attacked X5 by running with the ball directly at him within 35 yards of goal.

b. X6 on recognizing X5 is in a 1 v 1 situation in or near to a potential goal-scoring position should move to position himself in a covering position behind X5 and give information to X5 on how best to defend in this situation.

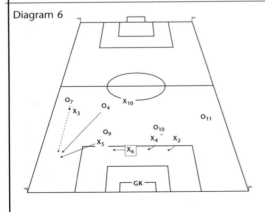

Diagram 6

6. <u>A marking defender leaves his immediate opponent to counter a bigger threat</u>

Situations

a. O4 (midfield) has moved into a flank position to receive a pass from O7 in a crossing area.

b. X5 recognizes the danger and leaves O9 to pressure O4 on receiving or having possession.

c. X6 now moves to mark O9 as appropriate and X4 and X2 adjust their roles.

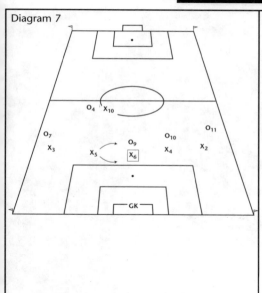

Diagram 7

7. <u>The opposition position an attacker against our sweeper</u>

Situations

a. O9 who was to be marked by X5 has positioned himself in front of the sweeper and plays there as an attacking tactic.

b. X6 may now take the following courses of action:
   - Mark O9 and X5 becomes sweeper
   - Position X5 in front of O9 and accept responsibility for O9.
   - Step up and attempt to catch O9 offside in crucial situations as appropriate.

X5 takes over the role of sweeper as often as possible.

SIMPLE PRACTICE SITUATIONS
TO
TEACH THE SWEEPER AND MARKERS

Practice One

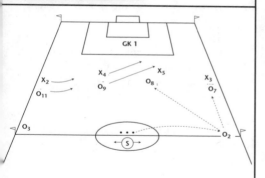

1. 4 attackers (O11, O7, O8, O9) v 4 markers (X4, X5) + 1 GK.
2. S passes to O2 or O3 to feed the strikers and then may support from rear positions and 'feed' their runs – attackers play to score past GK1.
3. Defenders on winning possession, play to deliver the ball to S, push up quickly, receive return pass and carry ball over halfway line.

Coaching Points
Marking:
1. Discipline concentration to man-mark opponent.
2. Marking quality – position, distance, stance.
3. Read the man on the ball, watch your opponent.
4. Intercept and break, spoil and recover, hold and stick to your opponent when he has possession.
5. Near-side marking, far-side marking

Practice Two

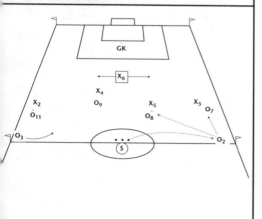

1. Organization as previous practice but now introduce X6 as 'sweeper'.
2. Attackers (O11, O8, O9, O7) play to score past GK1 and are support-ed from behind by O2 and O3.
3. Defenders objective is to gain pos-session and to break out and over the halfway line by possession play or deliver early to S and break quickly to support.

Coaching Points
Markers - as previous practice.
Sweeper - Positioning
a. Between the ball and the penalty spot as the ball moves across the field.
b. 10 yards behind the markers
c. FLAT - between the back markers, the nearer to the goal the more for-ward the opposition play.
d. In position to be first, if needed, to passes played behind the defense.

Practice Three

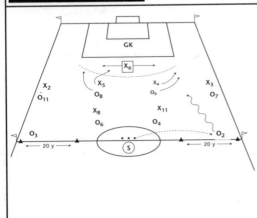

1. Organization as previous practice but now introduce 2 v 2 or 3 v 3 in midfield according to chosen strategy.
2. On gaining possession, defenders attack and score past one back player running with the ball over the halfway line between the cones indicated.

Coaching Points
Sweeper:
a. Positioning as above according to movement of the ball.
b. ROLE: communicating, organizing, reading the play.
c. Importance of 35 yard line (marked for him).

Markers: as previous practice
Midfield Players:
a. Marking roles
b. Pressuring roles
c. Covering wing-backs in 1 v 1.
d. Tracking runners to back of defense
e. Defending on takeovers, wall passes.

Practice Four

1. Organization as Practice Three but on receiving possession, (O2, O3) may <u>run the ball forward</u> or <u>pass to attackers</u> as appropriate.

Coaching Points
Sweeper:
Positioning:
a. As previous practices.
b. When and where to come forward to defend against attacking threats.
c. Support Markers (X5, X4) being attacked in 1 v 1 situations.
d. Positioning on crosses.
e. Importance of the 35 yard line.

Markers:
a. Discipline and quality of marking.
b. When tight, when loose marking.

Midfield:
a. Countering the runners from deep, e.g. O2, O3.
b. Covering wing backs.
c. Pressuring and defending in 1 v 1.

Practice Five

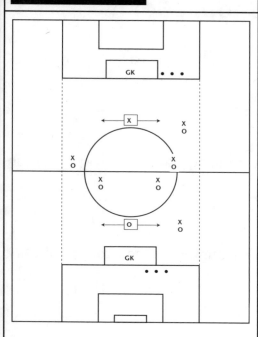

1. 8 v 8 on the field 44 yards wide x 80 yards long.
2. Two goalkeepers, 2 designated sweepers.
3. Free play except the sweeper has free touches in own half and restricted to two touches in the attacking half.

Coaching Points

Markers:
a. Position, stance, distance, read the play.
b. Intercept and break quickly.
c. Stay on feet and 'hold' opponents etc.

Sweeper:
a. <u>Positioning</u>
b. <u>Supporting</u> teammates in 1 v 1 within 30 yards of the goal.
c. <u>Communication</u> with other defenders.

<u>Attacking role</u> - pass, support, run with the ball on intercepting in the defensive half.

Practice Six

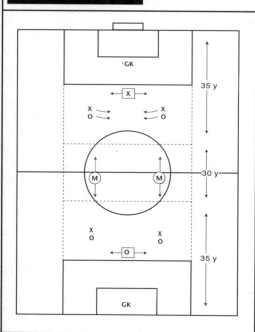

1. Each team has one goalkeeper, 1 sweeper, 2 markers and 2 strikers.
2. 2 MIDFIELD players have only 3 touch maximum in possession and basically <u>feed the strikers</u>.
3. Field is 44 yards wide x 100 yards long.
4. Players initially remain in zones - <u>later MIDFIELD players may attack if they pass into the ATTACKING THIRD or run the ball into the ATTACKING THIRD</u> - only 1 MIDFIELD player may attack.

Coaching Points
a. All previous points from earlier practices.

Later:
a. Introduce 2 wingers for each team who operate in attacking wide positions only.
b. Increase strikers/markers by 1

Sweeper Should Be:

1. **Composed and accurate** when reading the play.

2. **Thoughtful** when positioning.

3. **Decisive** when acting.

4. **Safe** when under pressure - never taking risks nor being caught in possession.

5. **Creative** if possible in possession.

6. Audible, **positive**, assertive and encouraging when communicating with co-defenders.

Coaching Books from REEDSWAIN

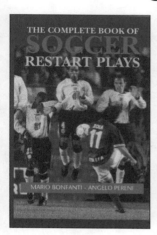
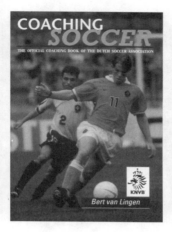

Coaching Books from REEDSWAIN

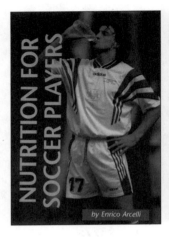
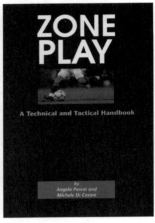
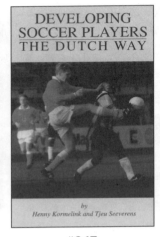

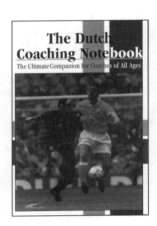

Coaching Books from REEDSWAIN

#291:
Soccer Fitness Training
by Enrico Arcelli
and Ferretto Ferretti
$12.95

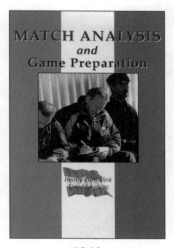

#261:
Match Analysis
and Game Preparation
Henny Kormelink and Tjeu Seevrens
$12.95

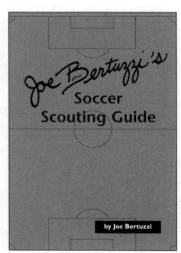

#789:
Soccer Scouting Guide
by Joe Bertuzzi
$12.95

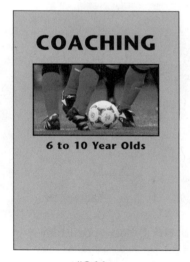

#264:
Coaching
6 to 10 Year Olds
by Giuliano Rusca
$14.95

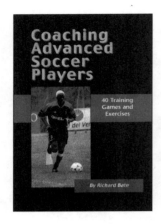
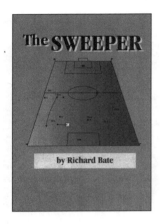